TOPICS TODAY

SO-AVI-888

Cyber Mobs, Trolls, and Online Harassment

By Kate Mikoley

Cavendish
Square

New York

Published in 2022 by Cavendish Square Publishing, LLC
29 E. 21st Street New York, NY 10010

Copyright © 2022 by Cavendish Square Publishing, LLC

First Edition

Website: cavendishsq.com

This publication represents the opinions and views of the author based on his or her personal experience, knowledge, and research. The information in this book serves as a general guide only. The author and publisher have used their best efforts in preparing this book and disclaim liability rising directly or indirectly from the use and application of this book.

Portions of this work were originally authored by Allison Krumsiek and published as *Cyber Mobs: Destructive Online Communities* (*Hot Topics*). All new material this edition authored by Kate Mikoley.

All websites were available and accurate when this book was sent to press.

Cataloging-in-Publication Data

Names: Mikoley, Kate.
Title: Cyber mobs, trolls, and online harassment / Kate Mikoley.
Description: New York : Cavendish Square, 2022. | Series: Topics today | Includes index.
Identifiers: ISBN 9781502661012 (pbk.) | ISBN 9781502661029 (library bound) | ISBN 9781502661036 (ebook)
Subjects: LCSH: Cyberterrorism–Juvenile literature. | Computer crimes–Juvenile literature. | Computer crimes–Prevention–Juvenile literature.
Classification: LCC HV6773.15.C97 M55 2022 | DDC 364.16′8–dc23

Editor: Kate Mikoley
Copyeditor: Nicole Horning
Designer: Deanna Paternostro

Some of the images in this book illustrate individuals who are models. The depictions do not imply actual situations or events.

CPSIA compliance information: Batch #CS22CSQ: For further information contact Cavendish Square Publishing LLC, New York, New York, at 1-877-980-4450.

Printed in the United States of America

Find us on

We the People

insure domestic Tranquility, provide for the c...

and our Posterity, do ordain and establish th...

Article. I.

Representatives shall be composed of Members chosen every second Year by

Section. 1. All legislative Powers herein granted shall be vested in a Congress of the United States, wh...

Section. 2. The House of Representatives shall be composed of Members chosen every second Year by the People of the several State Legisla...

No Person shall be a Representative who shall not have attained to the Age of twenty five Years...

Representatives and direct Taxes shall be apportioned among the several States which may be inc...

SOCIALIZING SAFELY

It's human nature to want to spend time with others. Whether it's through in-person contact, talking on the phone, writing letters, texting, or chatting online, being social is part of being human. Throughout history, humans have formed groups. These groups often form communities and help people feel connected.

Early on, groups were often formed as a means to get things done. While working together to achieve common goals is still an important part of socialization, there's a bigger reason people today form groups: friendship. You might belong to one friend group or have several different groups you socialize with. There are also many groups beyond friend groups, such as families, sports teams, religious groups, neighborhoods, and many more. In order for things to run smoothly, people need to be able to communicate in a healthy way with people both inside and outside of their own groups.

A Human Right

The ability to communicate with others and connect with them often depends on being able to speak freely. One of the most basic human rights that people around the world tend to agree

The First Amendment is part of the Bill of Rights, or the first 10 amendments to the U.S. Constitution. In addition to freedom of speech, the First Amendment also protects freedom of religion, freedom of the press, and the right to peacefully protest.

on is the freedom of speech. The First Amendment to the U.S. Constitution lays the foundation for Americans' right to free speech. It states that "Congress shall make no law ... abridging the freedom of speech."[1]

The Founding Fathers believed that the freedoms of speech, information, and ideas were key to having a healthy society. However, freedom of speech is much more complicated than just being able to say whatever you want, whenever you want. In general, the U.S. Supreme Court has found that free speech does not include speech that causes harm, such as shouting "fire" in a crowded building when there is no fire. The court has determined that this type of speech can be harmful and is not essential to liberty.

The idea that you have the freedom of speech except when that speech could cause harm may seem simple enough. However, there was no internet when the Bill of Rights was written, and the internet makes the idea of free speech a bit more complicated. Do the same rules apply to people typing on a keyboard that apply to people speaking aloud?

It's All Online

Thanks to the internet, it's now easier than ever to form and join groups with other people from all over the world. Forming groups like these can help people with common interests connect. They can also help people learn about and understand other points of view. However, people are not always so willing to learn. Sometimes, online groups lead to bullying—or worse.

A large group of angry or violent people is called a mob. Mobs often form quickly and can be difficult to control. They may harass or bully others who, generally, do not belong to the same group. Individuals who harass others online are known as trolls. Sometimes, a group of trolls will band together to form a cyber mob. A cyber mob is a group of people who band together to harass another person or group of people online. They're often doing so in response to things they've seen in the news or opinions of others that they disagree with.

Cyber mobs often use hate speech, threaten violence or attacks, and shame their victims. The trolls may be hiding behind computer screens, but their threats are real.

Once something is on the internet, it's hard to keep it private. Even if it's removed from the website it was posted on, it still exists. Sometimes, cyber mobs will make use of this by posting their victim's personal information. Certain information, such as addresses, phone numbers, and Social Security numbers, can put a person's life or well-being in danger when made public.

Other times, cyber mobs create their own, false information to harass someone. They may edit photos of the victim to make it look like they were doing something bad. They might also file false police reports to make the victim look bad. Once this false information is online, it can harm the victim for years to come. Employers or schools might see the information and believe it is true. This could affect whether the person gets a job or gets into a school.

This might all sound scary—and in many ways, it is—but there is hope when it comes to dealing with cyber mobs, trolls, and online harassment in general. Most social media websites have guidelines, called terms of service, which users agree to when signing up. If someone is being harassed on social media, it's likely the harasser is breaking these terms. If this is the case, they can be reported to the website, and then it is up to the people who run the website to decide what, if anything, they will do. Some social media websites block the harasser from being able to use the platform. Other times, their comments or posts may be removed or include a warning or advisement to viewers. Furthermore, many acts performed by cyber mobs, including threats of violence and stalking, are real crimes and should be reported to law enforcement.

WHEN THE INTERNET TURNS NEGATIVE

In 2019, 90 percent of adults in the United States used the internet in some capacity. With smartphones, many of these people have the internet with them all the time. This means the tools to communicate, learn, and find new ideas are often literally in the palms of their hands. Unfortunately, it also means the possibility of being harassed online is never too far away.

Today, more than half of the global population has an internet connection. This allows people from all over the world to connect with each other. Groups on the internet are often created around similarities, such as love of a common television show, musical group, or entertainer. Support groups are also formed online for people facing challenges such as cancer or the loss of a loved one. However, the internet also introduces people to ideas they may not like or people they may not agree with. Sometimes, people misuse this connection to harass those with different opinions or views. Often, people on the internet are harassed for the things they enjoy or simply for who they are. Many people do not feel safe sharing their ideas on the internet because of bullying like this.

Smartphones make it easy to connect with friends, but they also make it easy to be targeted by bullies.

In-Person versus Online Bullying

The feelings of fear, embarrassment, or pain that come from being bullied are the same whether the bullying takes place in person or online. However, if you're being bullied in person, you may be able to simply walk away. While this, of course, is not always the case with in-person bullying, it is never the case with online bullying, or cyberbullying. With cyberbullying, the abuse can follow someone wherever they go; the bully does not need to be physically present to make an impact on the victim.

Cyberbullying can also be repeated more often than regular bullying. If a bully in school writes a mean note to a target,

Cancel Culture

It's common these days to hear that a celebrity or other person in the public eye is "canceled." This means people stop supporting the person, often because of something they said or did. For example, in 2020, Twitter users "canceled" Lana Del Rey. She had posted on Instagram about being criticized for songs that people said did not empower women. Her post mentioned artists who she said sang about similar topics. Del Rey claimed that these artists did not get criticized for singing about the same kinds of things she did. Most artists she named were women of color. Many people thought it was wrong that she tore down these women to defend herself.

Often, a celebrity being "canceled" did something many or most people would agree is wrong or offensive. People may decide to stop listening to the person's music or watching their movies or TV shows. Everybody has the right to stop supporting a person in these ways, especially when they do something they believe is wrong. However, when a person is "canceled," cyber mobs often start harassing them online too. This can make the situation worse for all involved and can be potentially dangerous.

the target can throw the note away. Although the bully can always write a new one, they have certain limitations. In contrast, mean notes on the internet can be passed around forever, reproduced quickly, and brought back after being deleted. The same can happen with photos or videos. A cyber mob may take an embarrassing video of a victim and continue the harassment by posting it to different websites. New members of cyber mobs may discover the video years later and start the harassment all over again.

This kind of harassment and bullying can be unintended. A friend might take a funny or embarrassing photo of another

Some people believe "canceled" celebrities such as Lana Del Rey are simply facing the consequences of problematic actions.

friend and send it to them. Although both friends would know this was a joke, the image could be stolen by someone who was not in on the joke. It could then be used to bully and harass the subject of the picture. The bully may post the photo on multiple websites or send it to parents, teachers, or employers of the victim in an effort to get them in trouble or embarrass them. Anyone who helps spread the photo becomes part of the cyber mob. This can include people who know the victim as well as people who do not even know the person. In legal terms, these bystanders become accessories to any crime that happens related to the spread of the photo. However, this does not apply to people who try to help by sending the photo to teachers, parents, or the police. It only applies to those people who share it in an effort to hurt the victim. Some people may not even realize they are doing this; they may share the photo because they think it is funny, not thinking about the fact that the subject of the photo is a real person with real feelings. This is called dehumanizing, and it makes it easier for people to be cruel. Dehumanizing can happen either by accident or on purpose.

Freedom of Speech

Words shared online are protected by freedom of speech in many countries, including the United States, as well as by the United Nations (UN). It is a difficult balance for online communities to give everyone a right to their ideas while protecting vulnerable groups from harassment. It is important to note, however, that in the United States, the First Amendment protects people's speech and ideas from being censored by the government. Social media websites, which are where much online harassment takes place, are generally privately owned. This means they can, in fact, censor or remove harassing comments that people make. This is often a point of debate, especially when it comes to exactly what and how much is censored.

Cyber mobs aren't just on social media. They can be found all over the internet, from news websites to gaming platforms.

However, even on these privately-owned social media websites, not all harmful or harassing comments end up being removed. Even those that are taken down can still live on elsewhere on the internet, such as in the form of screenshots. In fact, there are many ways the internet and even freedom of speech laws have actually aided the rise of harassment in the form of cyber mobs.

Forming Cyber Mobs

Bullies exist in all communities, online and offline. Someone who is a bully may threaten a victim either physically or verbally. Bullies often spread rumors, or untrue information, about a victim. They sometimes act nice to a victim to get the victim to tell them a secret or embarrassing information. Later, the bullies will use that information against their victim.

Participation in a cyber mob is considered bullying behavior. Bullies online tend to seek out communities of other bullies. If someone who does not like another group of people finds a community of people who believe the same things they do, it can be easy for them to spread hateful information. In online communities, the bully may not even know the victim. Members of a cyber mob may not have anything personally against the victim, but a group may be able to convince others that the person deserves to be bullied for some reason. This may be because of skin color, gender, sexual orientation, or something the victim did that the group is reacting to in an inappropriately severe way. A group of people who attack other people can begin to think and act as a group even without ever seeing each other. They might temporarily forget their own ideas and follow the leader. This is called a mob mentality.

Another term for this mob mentality is groupthink. This term was coined by social psychologist Irving Janis and refers to groups that make bad decisions under social pressure. Janis studied groups and concluded that the social pressures in a group may lead individuals to act in immoral ways. He defined group-think as "a deterioration of mental efficiency, reality testing, and moral judgment that results from in-group pressures."[1]

In a 1973 *New York Times* article, Janis explained that while making decisions as a group can often be advantageous, "The advantages of having decisions made by groups are often lost because of psychological pressures that arise when the members work closely together, share the same values, and above all face a crisis situation in which everyone is subjected to stresses that generate a strong need for affiliation."[2]

The participants in a cyber mob form opinions based on unchallenged assumptions. They may think the target of their hate is bad because the rest of the group does. Even if someone challenges that idea, they may ignore certain facts rather than admit they might be wrong. Individuals involved in groupthink believe they are right even when shown evidence and arguments to prove they are not, and they use this sense of righteousness to excuse the group's or their own bad behavior. Groupthink can lead individuals to ignore the negative consequences of their actions and stereotype anyone outside the group as an enemy. When group members think they are right at all costs and that anyone who believes otherwise is an enemy, they can make dangerous decisions. Individuals within the group also have to be careful. In groupthink, there is no room for people to question the beliefs of the group. Individuals who begin to doubt the actions of the group may become targets of the group's hate or harassment themselves.

Online, it is even easier for people to fall into the mob mentality than it is in person. Some scientists believe that joining certain online communities makes it easier for a person to experience deindividuation, which is when a person forgets their personal views and moral compass and defers to the group. People in groups tend to forget what they know is right and wrong and follow the group instead. It can be difficult for someone who has never been caught up in groupthink to understand how this can happen, but psychologists understand that it is a real and serious problem. Deindividuation happens offline too. When a group begins to bully someone in a public place, it is hard for others to tell them to stop. Even people standing outside the group may feel a loss of their sense of right and wrong. It can be hard to speak up against bullies for fear of the group turning on them instead. This kind of deindividuation makes it easier for bullies to continue being cruel without punishment.

The internet also makes it easier to target people with hatred. This is how like-minded communities can sometimes become cyber mobs. Bullies will pick a target of their attacks and dehumanize the person, turning them into an enemy to be defeated. Sharing feelings or thoughts with a group makes bullies feel they are right even more strongly. The internet helps make these groups meaner. They use their anonymity, or the ability to hide their real names, as a tool for cyber abuse.

Hiding the Truth

Some websites allow users to be anonymous. Millions of people can interact online without knowing who the other people they're communicating with really are. In a face-to-face conversation, each person can see the effect of their words on the other person. Without these limitations, people online often feel uninhibited by social rules about politeness. This reduces empathy for people, which can make it easier to be mean. Several studies have shown that anonymity can increase the likelihood that people will form a mob mentality.

In a 2018 article for the Association for Psychological Science, writer Joe Dawson discussed several studies about anonymity and pointed out that the results don't always point directly one way or the other. He said:

> Behavioral studies on the role anonymity plays in online interactions have yielded mixed results. Overall, researchers have found that anonymity can reveal personality

traits that face-to-face interactions may hide, but that it also allows strong group rules and values to guide individual behavior.[3]

Anonymity online can make people more prone to behaving inappropriately or differently than they normally would. In an online space where users cannot be held personally responsible for their words, some people take the opportunity to be mean. A study from Stanford University found that people who write harassing comments tend to post more often when they receive negative feedback. Unlike most people, a troll might think it is fun to anger people.

After the hotly debated 2016 U.S. presidential election, Twitter finally stepped in to ban hate groups. Women and people of color had been reporting increasing threats for years on Twitter. Most of the accounts sending harassing tweets were anonymous. There were ways to block certain users but no way to make the harassment stop; members of cyber mobs simply created new Twitter profiles to harass someone. Twitter added new features that allowed users to report hateful language and targeted threats. It also worked to reduce the number of fake accounts that were used for harassment.

Many websites have restricted anonymity. To make comments on blogs or online articles, users may have to log in with their Facebook profile. This means their name and photo will be next to any comment they make. Some hope this will encourage people to remember that their words are permanent. They believe losing anonymity might stop some of the more hurtful comments. Still, many people set up Facebook profiles with fake names and photos, so this is not a completely effective way to restrict anonymity.

Some people believe the right to be anonymous is an important part of the internet and restricting anonymity is wrong. In a 1995 Supreme Court ruling, *McIntyre v. Ohio Elections*, the court stated, "Anonymity is a shield from the tyranny of the majority."[4] The Supreme Court found that being anonymous could help everyone share opinions without being punished for unpopular ones. On the internet, being anonymous can help people share and spread opinions that are not of the majority. In some areas of the world, these opinions may be against governments that do not protect the right to free speech. To protect the right to speak against these governments, anonymity is important.

However, some people use online anonymity to spread false information without facing consequences. During the COVID-19 pandemic and the months leading up to the 2020 presidential election, several websites, including Facebook and Twitter, removed posts that provided false information or flagged them with messages warning that the information in the posts might be misleading. False information, also known as misinformation, might not be directly harassing anyone, but the spread of misinformation online often helps or encourages cyber mobs to form. The subsequent harassment by cyber mobs often has to do with this misinformation.

During the COVID-19 pandemic, doctors and other medical experts advised the public on ways to stay safe and lessen the spread of the disease. Dr. Anthony Fauci was one of the most common faces people saw on television and other news outlets doing this. Dr. Fauci is a medical doctor and an expert in his field. He became the director of the National Institute of Allergy and Infectious Diseases (NIAID) in 1984 and maintained the role during the pandemic. This job means advising the president, and often the public, on important public health matters. During the COVID-19 pandemic, Dr. Fauci was also an important member of the White House Coronavirus Task Force. Dr. Fauci used his expertise in medicine and science to advise the public on safe practices during the pandemic. Meanwhile, Donald Trump, the president at the time, often downplayed the severity of the pandemic. Dr. Fauci's comments sometimes directly contradicted things President Trump was saying. Some of Trump's supporters took issue with this and

Dr. Fauci gave frequent reports on COVID-19 and became a well-known public figure. Unfortunately, he received death threats from people who didn't believe what he was saying.

From Cyber Mob to Real Mob

During his presidency, Donald Trump often took to Twitter to complain about people who didn't agree with him or spoke out against him. His supporters often backed him up and would take to Twitter or other social media websites themselves to post hateful, often harassing, comments at or about the people the president was speaking out against. When a well-known person spoke out against Trump, they would often be met with this kind of harassment by his followers, even if Trump himself never said anything about the person.

The Online Harassment Field Manual from PEN America uses the following as an example of a cyber-mob attack: "Ricochet editor and politically-conservative columnist Bethany Mandel experienced a surge of anti-Semitic trolling from self-identified white nationalists via Facebook and Twitter after publicly declaring her opposition to Donald Trump."[1]

At times, however, cyber mobs become real mobs. After Joe Biden won the 2020 presidential election, Trump falsely claimed Democrats, who he said stole the election, committed voter fraud—even though there was no evidence of this. Many of Trump's followers believed Trump's claims, and on the day Congress met to certify the Electoral College votes, which would confirm Biden's win, they stormed the U.S. Capitol in Washington, D.C., where Congress was meeting. The January 6, 2021, attack left at least five people dead.

1. "Defining 'Online Abuse': A Glossary of Terms," PEN America: Online Harassment Field Manual, onlineharassmentfieldmanual.pen.org/defining-online-harassment-a-glossary-of-terms/ (accessed January 26, 2021).

would post mean things about Dr. Fauci online. They also spread misinformation about the pandemic. Dr. Fauci has said that he even received death threats and members of his family were harassed too.

Often, the people spreading misinformation believe it to be true and do not realize the things they are sharing are incorrect and can be harmful. This is part of why it's very important to check where the information is coming from and do your own research before reposting anything online.

What's Protected?

Freedom of speech is important in a free society. If everyone can share their ideas and speak out about problems, then groups of people can work together to come up with solutions. Freedom of speech means everyone gets to voice their opinion, even opinions that other people may find hurtful or mean. There are some exceptions, however; threats of death or violence are not protected, and neither are libel or slander, which are lies deliberately spread to ruin a person's reputation.

Freedom of speech allows groups such as the Ku Klux Klan (KKK) to say negative, hateful, and cruel things about certain groups. In the case of the KKK, these remarks are often targeted at Black Americans. The First Amendment applies to statements made online as well as offline, so the KKK is allowed to have a website that promotes its hateful views. However, the First Amendment only protects people from punishment by the government. It does not guarantee that there will be no negative consequences to a person's statements. For instance, an employer who finds out one of their employees is a KKK member can choose to fire the employee if the workplace has a policy against engaging in hate speech. People are also free to disagree with others about their views; a school may block the KKK's website or a person may write a comment online speaking out against the KKK. Neither of these actions are a violation of the KKK's right to free speech.

Although freedom of speech applies both online and offline in the United States, there are still restrictions and consequences to hate speech. The United Nations (UN) defines hate speech as, "any kind of communication in speech, writing or behavior, that

Are You Informed?

Consent is an important topic. It means giving permission for someone to do something. If someone asks if they can take a photo of someone else and the person says yes, that person has given consent. Online, however, consent is not as easy to define. Consent is given when a user clicks OK on the terms and conditions of a website. By saying they have read the rules, they consent to obey them. In some of these rules, the website says it wants to use information or photos posted. Sometimes this is used to sell targeted ads or for promotional purposes. Many people do not read these rules before they click OK. Even if they do read the rules, they are often written in language that is difficult to understand. Although they are giving permission, they often do not know they have done it. Legally, however, the website is protected.

Agreeing without reading a document is still consent; however, it is not informed consent. Informed consent happens when someone has all the information necessary to make a good decision. Without understanding the terms of an agreement, a person cannot give informed consent. Without informed consent, a person might post something thinking it was private, only to have the website share it and possibly open them up to attacks from trolls or cyber mobs.

attacks or uses pejorative or discriminatory language with reference to a person or a group on the basis of who they are, in other words, based on their religion, ethnicity, nationality, race, color, descent, gender or other identity factor."[5]

Hate speech is protected by the First Amendment, but "fighting words" are not. Fighting words are words with no social value that are likely to cause harm or a breach of peace. In other words, if words spoken to a victim would make any reasonable person react with violence, these are fighting words. It can be difficult to prove whether something can be considered fighting words,

Social media websites are often places where hate groups—groups that are formed because of a shared hatred for another group of people—can engage in hate speech toward victims.

and different people have different views on this. Some believe all hateful speech should be banned, while others think the term "fighting words" only refers to direct threats of violence. When people bring a case to court, the court generally weighs the evidence and decides on a case-by-case basis whether a statement falls under the category of fighting words.

In the United States, everyone has the right to freedom of speech, and those who are victims of hate speech also have the right to speak up. Those targeted by hate speech on websites or social media can speak out against the cruel mobs and expose the authors. By reporting hate speech online, other users can help restrict the spread of these ideas. Many social media platforms, such as Facebook and Twitter, try to create a balance between promoting free speech for all ideas and becoming a place for hate to spread. It is not easy to balance the two.

Spreading Hate and Personal Data

In exchange for free access to social media, websites collect data on each user. Data collected by social media websites includes names, locations, friends lists, workplaces, and dates of birth. If this data falls into the wrong hands, it can be used for harassment. When a cyber mob focuses on an individual, they often look online for more information about the person. Even when users of social media websites make their information private, it is easy for good hackers to gain access to information. Trolls may then take this private information and use it to harass someone. For example, they may publicly post a person's address online and encourage people to vandalize the house.

Not all cyber mobs begin on social media. Other kinds of websites have been created to share the names, home addresses, pictures, and other personal information of people from certain groups that those creating the websites do not like. These websites may call for trolls to harass the people listed, whether or not they have actually done anything wrong. Acting on false information can lead people to commit crimes or target innocent people because they believe they are doing the right thing. Even if someone is actually guilty of wrongdoing, however, it is never acceptable for people to commit acts of violence or cruelty against them.

Protest versus Harassment

Sometimes, people use legitimate forms of protest in conjunction with harassment. One example of this was in the 2021 Capitol riots, when many people at first peacefully assembled to protest something they believed was wrong. After a while, however, the protests turned violent and people stormed the Capitol, committing various illegal acts.

People online can also take a legitimate form of protest and turn it into harassment. In 2015, Reddit users created a petition to get the CEO of Reddit, Ellen Pao, fired after a popular employee was fired and Pao banned several groups that were using the website to harass others and spread hate. Creating a petition is a legitimate form of protest, but the Reddit users also used trolling and harassing behavior. They created hateful photos and shared Pao's private information. In response to this treatment, Pao resigned, but she has remained vocal about eliminating online harassment. She wrote in a *Washington Post* article, "After making these policy changes to prevent and ban harassment, I, along with several colleagues, was targeted with harassing messages, attempts to post my private information online and death threats. These were attempts to demean, shame and scare us into silence."[6]

That is often the case with trolls and cyber mobs: They try to scare their victims in an effort to suppress points of view they don't agree with. At first, they may not even think their actions are harmful or constitute harassment, but things can escalate very

In addition to speaking out against online harassment, Ellen Pao has also spoken out against gender discrimination in the workplace.

quickly when a hateful group forms online. Even when social media users know each other, it can be easier to say cruel things when they are not face to face. Social media allows other users to "favorite" or "like" a post. When something cruel is said and other users show support for it, the original poster feels justified in their view. This can lead them to continue to say cruel things, thinking that if the mob agrees, it must be a true statement or something good. Some of these mean posters do not consider the feelings of their target; others get enjoyment out of hurting them.

Your Opinion Matters!

1. Have you ever been harassed online? If so, how did it make you feel? If not, how do you think it would make you feel?

2. Have you ever acted as a troll online? If so, did you think it was harmful at the time? Would you handle things differently now?

3. Do you think it violates freedom of speech when social media websites censor or remove harmful content?

MANY METHODS OF HARASSMENT

Harassment and bullying can generally be grouped into three main types: verbal, social, and physical. Verbal harassment includes teasing, name-calling, inappropriate comments, and threatening to harm or hurt someone. While the word "verbal" often refers to words spoken out loud, it really just has to do with the use of words, so most online harassment is considered verbal harassment, even though it is commonly written rather than spoken aloud.

Social bullying or harassment happens when someone hurts a person's relationships with others or harms their reputation. This can be done by excluding or leaving a person out of activities or groups on purpose, spreading rumors so others exclude them from groups, purposely embarrassing them in public, or telling other people to be mean to them. Often, a group will use this type of bullying to make the group members feel more connected. By excluding someone, the people not excluded feel special. Social harassment can happen online too. Publicly posting embarrassing photos or stories about a person on social media or encouraging others to post mean comments online can be considered social harassment or bullying.

◄ Spreading rumors about a person online can affect their relationships in real life too.

Physical harassment is when someone hits, kicks, pushes, trips, or punches a victim. Physical bullying can also involve breaking something that someone else owns or stealing items that are important to them. At worst, this type of harassment can include sexual assault or rape, murder, and even causing someone to die by suicide. Although someone cannot physically harm another person online, cyber mobs sometimes make posts online encouraging people to physically attack a victim. They may also tell the victim to hurt themselves or others.

Cyber mobs may harass their victims both online and in person. They gather information about a target, often using both legal and illegal means. They may hack into someone's private network to steal information (theft), publish false information about someone (libel), stalk their victims (criminal harassment), and use speech that includes threats or name-calling (verbal harassment). Cyber mobs and trolls can use one or more of these tactics to bully or harass someone.

Often, cyber mobs claim that their harassment is just an exercise of their free speech. Some of the harassment could qualify as fighting words, but there is not generally punishment for using the words online. Social media bullies and trolls might be blocked or have their account deleted, but often only if someone reports them. Typically, the only words online that are taken seriously by law enforcement are called "true threats." This is when someone makes a threat to kill or otherwise hurt someone and a reasonable person would take the threat seriously. When a victim of cyber harassment feels afraid for their safety, the law has more ways to get involved.

No Escape

Even though harmful bullying takes place in person, too, online harassment can escalate more quickly and be harder to get away from. It can be easier for anonymous bullies to target someone in all parts of their life. Cyber mobs may form on one social

Defining Cyberbullying

StopBullying.gov defines cyberbullying as "bullying that takes place over digital devices like cell phones, computers, and tablets. Cyberbullying can occur through SMS, Text, and apps, or online in social media, forums, or gaming where people can view, participate in, or share content."[1]

Sharing negative, mean, or untrue things about a person is considered cyberbullying even if the information is not sent directly to that person. For example, the information may be posted publicly or sent to people who know the victim in an attempt to get them to exclude or attack the victim. According to a report by the Cyberbullying Research Center, one in five kids between ages nine and twelve has been a part of cyberbullying, whether they've been the victim, the bully, or a witness. The report also notes that among teens, "those who have been cyberbullied – as well as those who cyberbully others – are more likely to struggle academically, emotionally, psychologically, and even behaviorally."[2]

Every state has their own laws regarding bullying. These laws require schools to respond to the bullying in some way. Today, many states include cyberbullying in these laws. Even if a state doesn't include cyberbullying in their anti-bullying laws, schools can discipline the bullies through their own school or local policies.

1. "What Is Cyberbullying?" StopBullying.gov, July 21, 2020, www.stopbullying.gov/cyberbullying/what-is-it.

2. Justin W. Patchin and Sameer Hinduja, "Tween Cyberbullying in 2020," Cyberbullying Research Center in Partnership with Cartoon Network, i.cartoonnetwork.com/stop-bullying/pdfs/CN_Stop_Bullying_Cyber_Bullying_Report_9.30.20.pdf (accessed January 26, 2021).

media platform but can transition to other platforms. For instance, people may start harassing someone through Twitter and eventually move to Facebook, TikTok, or Instagram as well.

Through these platforms, bullies can find where the target goes to school, lives, or works. If the victim has a job, the bullies may even create false posts on business websites such as Yelp to make the person look bad at their job, get them in trouble at work, or give their company a bad name. People's connected online profiles can provide cyber mobs with easy access to both their personal and professional lives.

There are many groups and campaigns that work to stop online bullying. While the important thing is to find ways to stop the bullies from harassing their victims, there are also ways the victims can respond to the bullying to make sure the situation doesn't get worse and ensure their own safety. Ross Ellis, founder of STOMP Out Bullying said:

> If a teen is being harassed online, the worst thing they can do is to respond. They should delete the post and block the person. If a teen is being threatened, on or offline, parents should be told immediately so they can report this to law enforcement. Text threats [or] posts should be printed out. These should be brought to the attention of law enforcement by the teen's parents. Once it is brought to law enforcement, posts and texts should be deleted and blocked.[1]

Trolling Is No Joke

Sometimes, trolls think their actions are all in good fun. They may say they're just joking around. However, to the victim, these events are not fun, and they're certainly not funny. In face-to-face communication, people learn to read social cues such as facial expressions, body language, or eye movement. These cues help people understand how someone else feels. For instance, if the person they are talking to does not make eye contact, it may be clear they are uncomfortable. This helps people understand that they should ask questions or change the subject. On the internet, people cannot see these social cues. Since most things on the internet are expressed in words or images alone, they also miss out on tone of voice. One person may read a post as a joke, while another person may see the same post as serious.

People sometimes lose their sense of reality online. Offline, trolls might be concerned with what others think. They might be able to read social cues and participate in society in appropriate ways. However, they may believe that being online frees them from consequences. Without social cues, trolls may lose the inhibition that comes from seeing someone face to face. Inhibitions keep people from doing harmful or dangerous things. They are the unconscious feeling that someone should not do something. Inhibitions may stop someone from saying something mean.

Researchers believe trolls think too much about themselves. They may want to attract attention and do not care if the attention is negative. Trolls may give their target a set of made up qualities. Instead of knowing someone as a person, a troll may see them as an obstacle. Trolls tend to believe the internet is a game they have to win. Winning happens by outsmarting other people and "destroying" them with words and images.

Trolls want to feel more powerful or better than others. They may lie about who they are; for example, they may make up stories about how they are rich and famous or popular. In reality, many trolls are people who have been bullied themselves. They are often left out of groups, so they go online to feel accepted. Trolls may also take out their anger about their own problems on people online. Because they lose their inhibitions, trolls feel they can say whatever they want.

Studies of trolls have found that many of them enjoy making other people suffer. They find it fun to cause other people harm. This is called sadistic or psychopathic behavior. The worst trolls feel no remorse or guilt for hurting other people. Wanting to hurt other people is not normal; psychologists call it anti-social behavior.

When a group of people who do not care about the feelings of others get together, they will hurt other people just to impress members of the cyber mob. This status-seeking is similar to attention-seeking behavior.

Cyber mobs often form online around trolling behavior. Trolling starts most often with a reaction to an idea or comment shared online. Trolling is when someone purposely harasses or antagonizes someone online by starting fights or intentionally upsetting others. This is often done by posting inflammatory messages. Trolls purposely say mean or controversial things with the intention of hurting the victim and getting them to react. Trolls may then try to get other people to feel sorry for them so more people will also post cruel things to the victim. They often trick other people into joining or forming a cyber mob.

When several trolls find each other online, they can quickly become a cyber mob. Cyber mobs and trolls may harass victims for ideas that are different. However, an individual troll may start provoking someone online for no good reason. Trolls often choose to mock personal characteristics of a target. These include race, ethnicity, gender, and sexuality. Women, especially women of color, are a favorite target of trolling behavior. Trolls may make crude comments about a person's body, claim a target has a sexually transmitted disease, or state someone has sex with many people. Their goal is to get other people angry enough to become a cyber mob.

Instead of writing thoughtful comments for or against an online article, trolls use threatening language and abusive comments. They often focus on the personal characteristics of the writer instead of the merits of an online argument. In this way, trolls make hateful speech personal. Sometimes, trolls are responding to things they find offensive. People have every right to disagree with others, but a troll's response does not simply explain why they disagree or think the other person is wrong; it instead attacks the victim in ways that often don't even have anything to do with the issue that brought about the conflict. For example, if a person posted a negative review of a restaurant that they didn't like, readers might reasonably respond explaining that

Even if you don't actively take part in harassing someone online, showing a troll's posts to others helps spread their message and could still have a negative impact on the victim.

they disagree and stating why they do like the restaurant. A troll, however, might respond by attacking the writer's physical appearance or intelligence. These are things that have nothing to do with what the writer said. Perhaps the troll is friends with the owner of the restaurant and is offended that this person doesn't like it. They have every right to feel upset, but that does not justify such a response.

Art Markman, a professor of psychology at the University of Texas at Austin, has noted that online comments are often "extraordinarily aggressive, without resolving anything."[2] In that way, these comments can be hurtful, but they don't offer any value or steps toward solving an issue or even getting a person to change their point of view.

"It's valuable to allow all sides of an argument to be heard. But it's not valuable for there to be personal attacks, or to have messages with an extremely angry tone. Even someone who is making a legitimate point but with an angry tone is hurting the nature of the argument, because they are promoting people to respond in kind," Markman said. "If on a website comments are left up that are making personal attacks in the nastiest way, you're sending the message that this is acceptable human behavior."[3]

Mean Memes and Vicious Videos

Sometimes, pictures and videos are taken without someone's knowledge and posted online without their permission. Other times, they are put on the internet by the people in them and later used for hurtful purposes by others. Once information is posted on the internet, the person who posted it no longer has any control over its use. Every photo uploaded to a website or an app is available for other people to find and use. Even if you think a photo is uploaded privately, there may be ways for others to access it.

Many memes are created using personal photos. Sometimes, these memes are real photos of people who do not know their

Online harassment should always be reported to a trusted adult. However, it may also be helpful to talk to a friend about it.

photo is being used for this purpose. Memes and other pictures of real people are often used in a joking fashion by people online. These jokes can become cruel quickly and can spread throughout the internet. Trolls and other cyber mob participants do not see the real pain caused by cruel memes. Victims of these meme campaigns often find out about the use of their pictures much later. Because the picture has been shared so many times, it can be difficult to find out who is responsible. Since the picture is often in many places, it can be impossible to have it removed from the internet. Victims of bullying through memes are often affected offline as well.

Lizzie Velásquez was born with a rare condition called Marfanoid-progeroid-lipodystrophy syndrome. It affects the structure of her face and keeps her from being able to gain weight. As a child, she was often bullied for her appearance. When she got older, someone made a YouTube video showing Velásquez and calling her "the world's ugliest woman." The video went viral, and strangers from around the world shared it and wrote mean comments. Some even told her she should end her own life. Rather than letting the hurt these trolls caused define her, Velásquez spoke out and stood up for herself. She started her own YouTube channel and became a motivational speaker.

In 2020, Velásquez was once again the victim of cruelty on the internet. Users on TikTok started doing something called the "New Teacher Challenge." These videos involved adults showing their children a photo of a person they claimed was their new teacher. In reality, the people in the photos were not the children's teachers. They were people who the parents decided looked different from what they considered "normal" or "standard." Sometimes the photos were mugshots. Other times, they showed people with disabilities. Many showed Lizzie Velásquez. Generally, the child in the video would react by being scared or shocked by the photo they were shown. Then, the parent would laugh, eventually telling the child it was a joke. Perhaps some of the parents did not fully think about this, but of course, the

Lizzie Velásquez is active on social media, where she often reminds people to be kind and embrace things that make them different.

people in these photos were real people, and these videos were cruel and hurtful. Velásquez said they also taught the children it is OK to laugh at people who do not look like you. She took to TikTok herself to respond to these hateful videos: "If you are an adult who has a young human in your life, please do not teach them that being scared of someone who doesn't look like them is OK, please ... we are humans. We have feelings."[4]

Harassing by Hacking

To harass people online, individual members of a cyber mob may use hacking to gain more information or access to a person's internet accounts. Hacking is defined as interrupting or changing normal network connections. A network is how computers connect to the internet. When hackers get into the connection, they can steal information. Hackers can gain access to things such as the login and password to social media accounts, health records, school records, and even banking websites.

Once a hacker has stolen login information, they have as much access to people's accounts as the owner of the account. Using this information, a hacker can change someone's password, locking them out. Then they can pretend to be the person and post content the victim would not normally say. No one would know for sure just from looking at the website or social media profile that a different person was posting, and it is difficult to prove that someone else has posted using their profile. This can cause embarrassing or hurtful things to be said in someone's name. Again, the goal is to get others so angry that they lose their inhibitions and join together to become a cyber mob.

Hackers may also use stolen information to ruin someone's finances. By stealing credit card or Social Security numbers, they can make purchases in someone else's name. There are ways the victim can prove they did not make the pruchases, but often, this is a difficult and time-consuming process. It may take quite a while to get their money back. Keeping personal information

Realizing your personal information has been stolen can be scary. Quickly reporting the theft and any fraud that has been committed can help resolve the situation.

private is important for protection both online and offline, so learning and practicing online safety skills is essential.

Cyberbullies will often use stolen information to copy photos or personal texts and emails. They may try to use this information to embarrass the victim. Everyone says things in private they might not want other people to know. By hacking into an email account, the cyberbullies can find emails and photos that a victim might not want other people to see. The bullies can then spread these private documents online to make others want to target the victim.

Sometimes, cyberbullies do not need to use computer or network hacking to steal information. They may get a cyber mob started to harass the victim until they release private information. These trolls manipulate, or control forcefully, to get what they want. The victim might release information under this pressure and then feel guilty. They might not report manipulation because they feel they gave in to bullies, even though it is not their fault.

Doxing

Once a cyber mob gains access to a victim's personal information such as a home address or phone number, they will typically intensify their attacks. Trolls may publish the personal information of a target. This unauthorized sharing of private information is called doxing. "Dox" is short for documents. Sometimes doxing is known as "dropping dox" because it involves exposing people's personal documents. Some doxed information may be easy to find, such as Facebook photos or an email address. Other information could be a Social Security number, an address, or other private information that generally requires hacking to find.

Doxing is often done to make a victim scared enough to do or stop doing something. Sometimes, a troll will respond to an argument on the internet with the home address of someone they want to silence. The post often includes a threat. Doxing is wrong; it is an attack on a specific person to get them to be quiet about their ideas or to feel fear. When doxing exposes information that is not part of the public record, it is a crime. Even if the doxed information is public record, such as arrest or divorce records, many people consider it unethical.

When one member of a cyber mob doxes information, it is often seen by other members of the mob as permission to use this personal contact information to continue harassing the target. Doxers may feel as though their victim deserves it. Even if the victim did do something wrong, they do not deserve to be harassed or have their personal information exposed.

Cyberstalking

Trolls will sometimes stalk people, both online and offline. Stalkers become obsessed with their victim. They often try to control the target. The stalker will try to follow the target and find out where they are at all times. They might also try to get the victim alone by spreading rumors to friends and family that make them think the victim wants to be alone or is too mean to hang out with anymore.

Cyberstalking is using technology to harass someone repeatedly. This can include sending many emails or text messages, going to multiple websites to post about someone in a mean way, and spreading rumors online. Some cyberstalkers will create new websites just to say cruel things about their victim. They may use a tactic called Google bombing, which is when a person makes all of the bad or untrue posts about a target show up first in a Google search. They can do this by hyperlinking all the posts across different websites. When Google or another search engine looks for information, the first results it displays are the ones that show up the most.

Many cyberstalkers try to start a cyber mob by making false accusations about a victim and asking other people to help shame or punish them. These accusations could be that the victim has committed a serious crime or that the victim is the one saying mean things about other people.

Sometimes cyberstalkers make true threats that the police treat seriously. There is no legal test to determine whether something is a true threat, so police look at the context. They will take into account things such as whether the two people know each other, whether the target seemed scared by the threat, and whether the person making the threat has a history of violence.

True threats may include specific details such as how and when a person or their family will be hurt or killed. They might mention where the person lives and how they are being watched. Law enforcement should take true threats seriously. In the United States, cyberstalking is a federal crime. Cyberstalkers can receive punishments such as prison time and monetary fines.

The first case of cyberstalking to result in death and go to trial involved a divorced couple. Christine Belford divorced her husband David Matusiewicz and was seeking custody of their three children. Matusiewicz used cyberstalking and other trolling behavior to try to stop her from gaining custody. He and his parents and sister formed a cyber mob. They posted fake stories on the internet claiming that Belford was abusing the children. They hacked into her Facebook account and used it to write horrible things. They would send messages to the court and child protective services against Belford.

Belford told police and her lawyers about the cyberstalking and abuse. The cyber mob continued to harass her. It expanded to include other people in her community. These people believed the lies Matusiewicz and his relatives had posted, so they became angry enough to harass Belford, feeling that she deserved it. A court hearing was scheduled in 2013 to settle the cyberstalking charges. At the courthouse, her former father-in-law shot and killed Belford and her friend Laura Beth Mulford. Belford's ex-husband and family were convicted of cyberstalking and murder.

Swatting

Another way people harass others using technology is swatting. SWAT stands for "special weapons and tactics." A SWAT team is a specially trained police unit that handles seriously dangerous situations. Swatting is when someone falsely reports an emergency in order to get police or a SWAT team to come to a location where no crime is actually happening. The swatter uses special technology to hide their phone number and reports a serious crime such as an active shooter or a hostage situation, making it likely the response will be serious. They say the crime is happening at an address where their victim is, such as their home or business. The swatter may have already known this information, or they could have found it through hacking, doxing, or cyberstalking. The police believe there is a real crime, so they enter the location with force, often with their guns drawn. The people inside have no idea what's going on, so this can be a very scary situation.

Some swatters think they are just pranking their victim. Others do it to harass someone they think deserves it. No matter what the intention is, swatting is wrong and can have serious repercussions. Not only is the police or SWAT team wasting time that could be used responding to real crimes, but swatting has also led to death. In 2017, 28-year-old Andrew Finch was killed by police entering his home. The police thought they were responding to a homicide and hostage situation, but in reality, a swatter had reported this false incident. The swatter was sentenced to 20 years in prison.

Speaking Out

Sadly, many victims of cyber mobs feel their only option is to stay quiet or hide from their harassers. Still, others, like Lizzie Velásquez, find the courage to speak up. By doing this, these people are helping others who may be unable to speak up or defend themselves.

A SWAT team can be a scary sight. Members of the team wear special protective gear and carry guns. At the least, a victim of swatting will be very frightened. At worst, someone could be killed.

After a school shooting in Parkland, Florida, several students who survived the shooting publicly called for stronger gun control laws in the United States. Some people who were against these potential laws banded together in cyber mobs to harass these students. They began making threats, posting cruel comments, and even promoting conspiracy theories that said these students were actually actors, rather than the truth, which was that they were survivors of a horrific school shooting. One of these students was David Hogg. After Hogg posted online about being rejected from several colleges, conservative news host Laura Ingraham made fun of him, causing more trolls to follow suit. Rather than staying quiet, Hogg spoke out. Soon, Ingraham had lost many of her sponsors. In an interview, Hogg said, "No matter who somebody is, no matter how big or powerful they may seem, a bully is a bully and it's important that you stand up to them."[5]

Your Opinion Matters!

1. Why is cyberbullying harder to get away from than in-person bullying?
2. How can memes be used by cyber mobs to hurt a victim?
3. How can cyberstalking threaten a person's life?

ONLINE ACTIONS, REAL CONSEQUENCES

Members of cyber mobs often do not think of themselves as trolls who are causing real harm to real people. They may think they are just joking around. However, their actions can have devastating consequences for their victims. As a result of online harassment, targets can miss out on opportunities such as jobs and getting into colleges. Their stolen personal information may be difficult to remove from the internet and can continue causing them problems for years to come. In some instances, people even lose their lives as a result of online harassment. Hiding behind a screen can make it easier for a bully to think their actions won't cause problems in real life, but this isn't true. Online actions have real and serious consequences. Most people know it's important to think about the consequences of their actions before they do something. It's important to do this when communicating and interacting with people online as well.

Most cyberbullying involving children and teens comes from other kids at their school. Like bullying offline, cyberbullying can ruin friendships. Friends may stop hanging out with or talking to the victim at school because they fear

◀ Victims of cyberbullying often feel isolated and alone.

their friendship will cause them to become victims too. This can make the victim feel even worse than they already do. Even though their former friends aren't the ones bullying them, their distancing can make the victim feel like they don't have anyone on their side. Victims of cyberbullying may lose trust in the people around them who do not help them stand up against the bullies.

School-Related Bullying

Many schools provide information to students and teachers about bullying and cyberbullying. People are more aware of the issue than ever before. However, according to StopBullying.gov,

Harassing a Hunter

A Minnesota dentist named Walter Palmer was the victim of a cyber mob in 2015, after he went on a hunt in the African country of Zimbabwe. He is believed to have paid $54,000 to go on the hunt, where he killed a lion named Cecil. This happened just outside of a national park. Cecil was well-known and loved by park visitors. After news spread that Palmer killed Cecil, people around the world became very angry, and many posted online about it. They were upset that he had seemingly killed an animal just to take it home as a trophy. This is known as trophy hunting. Many people around the world are against trophy hunting, and it is legal in many places, including Zimbabwe.

Some people claimed Palmer had not followed the necessary steps to make the hunt legal. However, officials eventually said Palmer's hunt was performed legally. Still, a cyber mob began to call for people to harass him. Many started calling his dental office and leaving threatening messages. Trolls posted false bad reviews of his dental practice. Many called for him to lose his practice completely.

about 20 percent of students in the United States between 12 and 18 years old report having experienced bullying. Among those who said they were bullied at school, around 15 percent said they were bullied online or by text.

At one middle school in Connecticut, an anonymous student created a Facebook page called Let's Start Drama and encouraged other students to send gossip or rumors. The owner of the page, who earned the nickname "Drama Queen" from writer Emily Bazelon, then spread the gossip and encouraged bullying at school. More than 500 local teenagers were actively spreading rumors and bullying other kids through the page. The conflict continued at school, with some students getting

The First Amendment protects people's right to protest, as long as they do not break other laws or rules while doing it. Many people legally protested Palmer's actions. However, some went beyond this, such as by threatening him.

into physical fights over things that had been posted on the page. A school official reported it to Facebook twice, hoping the website would disable it. Although the page broke Facebook's terms of service in several different ways, including the fact that "Drama Queen" was using a fake email account and that the page promoted bullying, the page stayed up until Bazelon, who wrote about the story for *The Atlantic*, went to Facebook headquarters to see why. The reporter found that the people on Facebook's Hate and Harassment Team had to deal with so many requests each day that sometimes they made mistakes and left up a page that should have been taken down. Let's Start Drama was deleted by Facebook after the reporter showed it to the Hate and Harassment Team, but this shows that users cannot always count on Facebook or other social media websites to help them fight cyber mobs.

Cyberbullying can have severe effects for victims. They may have trouble concentrating in school and begin to suffer psychological problems, such as depression and anxiety. These conditions can stay with a person into adulthood. If the information is not deleted, it will always be available for a person to look at online. This includes future friends, employers, and partners of the victim.

Cyberbullying can have consequences for the bullies as well. Many schools have created rules against cyberbullying. Bullies can get suspended from school, lose their place on sports teams or in clubs, and even face legal trouble if their actions break the law. People with jobs can get fired from their workplace for cyberbullying.

Emotional Issues

Bullying and cyber attacks can cause serious emotional problems for victims. Some victims of cyber mobs turn to alcohol or drug abuse. Many develop depression and anxiety. Victims with depression might stay in bed and miss school or work. Some

Impacting Others

Even people not directly involved with online harassment can be impacted by it. Seeing so much hate online can cause post-traumatic stress disorder (PTSD) symptoms even in people who are not the target of a cyber mob. According to a study by the Pew Research Center, 73 percent of people said they had witnessed someone else being bullied online. Being reminded of the cruelty people are capable of can make people feel fearful without being the direct target of these words, especially if the statements could be applied to them as well. For instance, a woman who sees anti-woman messages directed at a different woman may still feel upset. Researchers and community activists who study online abuse can be affected as well. While it is a good idea to think about things before posting them online, witnessing a cyber mob attack may make people afraid to post even harmless messages.

Parents also worry that their children will be bullied online. According to another study from the Pew Research Center, 59 percent of parents surveyed said they worried at least somewhat about their teenage child being harassed or bullied online.

victims develop anger problems or try to go out of their way to please everyone to prevent further bullying.

Victims of cyber mobs feel real fear from the cruel words they see on the screen. "Psychiatric injury, however, is but one possible harmful result of being mobbed," wrote Dr. Kenneth Westhues, a professor who studies mob behavior. "Some mobbing targets keep their sanity but succumb to cardiovascular disease—hypertension [high blood pressure], heart attack, or stroke. Most suffer loss of income and reputation. Marital breakdown and isolation from friends and family are also common outcomes."[1]

Defaming and Shaming

Cyber mobs often cause damage to someone's reputation, which is the shared ideas about a person based on outside information. When people hear and believe negative rumors, they form a negative opinion of the person they are hearing these statements about. Making such statements is called defamation of character. Defamation does not involve simply insulting someone, especially if the insult is an opinion. To count as defamation, the statement must have four qualities, according to Nolo, a website that aims to make difficult legal concepts easier for the average person to understand. Someone who is trying to prove defamation of character must be able to show that the statement was:

Published: The statement was written down (libel) where other people could see it or spoken (slander) where other people could hear it.

False: The statement must be able to be proven false with concrete evidence, otherwise the statement is not considered to be damaging. For example, saying that someone robbed a bank when they did not is something that can be proven false by an investigation.

Injurious: The statement must be damaging to the person's reputation. The person must be able to prove that they suffered in some way from the statement, such as being fired from a job or expelled from school.

Unprivileged: In certain rare circumstances, people's right to free speech is protected even when they defame someone. This generally only applies to lawmakers and people who testify in court.

Defamation can have serious consequences for the target. People with a bad reputation are often deemed untrustworthy.

Ruining a person's reputation can cause them to lose friends, job opportunities, scholarships, and more. To help people protect themselves, the Supreme Court has ruled that people can sue others for defamation, or take them to court to clear their name and hold the other person accountable for their actions. The Court said reputation law protects "the essential dignity and worth of every human being—a concept at the root of any decent system of ordered liberty."[2]

Cyber mobs often defame their targets. Sometimes, this is on purpose, but other times, people spread a rumor believing it is true, then find out it is false. Whether they do it on purpose or by accident, the consequences are the same for the victim, which is why people should always do their own research before sharing something negative.

Conspiracy theories and fake news reports are one way innocent people are sometimes victimized by defamation and cyber mobs. One well-known example of this is referred to as PizzaGate. Before the 2016 presidential election, a false claim that important members of the Democratic Party, including 2016 presidential candidate Hillary Clinton, were involved in a child trafficking ring made its way around the internet. People used an online message board called 4chan to spread their false ideas that a pizzeria in Washington, D.C., called Comet Ping Pong, was used as a front for the ring (which did not really exist).

Although there was no truth behind the story, it spread quickly on the internet. The lies made their way around social media sites such as Twitter, Facebook, and Reddit. They also were on websites that at first glance seem to look like regular news websites, but are actually used to spread fake news. A cyber mob attacked the pizzeria owner and others who worked there, sometimes sending them death threats. In December 2016, things turned from online harassment to physical danger. A man named Edgar M. Welch entered Comet Ping Pong and fired a military-style assault rifle. He said he was investigating the conspiracy theory, which he had believed

After the PizzaGate shooting, several websites removed posts and accounts that spread the conspiracy theory, but the damage was done. Workers at Comet Ping Pong were traumatized by the event.

was true. Luckily no one was hurt, but this could have been a tragic event.

In 2017, Welch was sentenced to four years in prison. The PizzaGate theory was disproven even before the shooting. Yet in 2020, people online were still pushing the theory. QAnon is a similar but broader unfounded conspiracy theory that falsely alleges a powerful group of people in government, business, and the media are running a child trafficking ring. QAnon supporters also spread ideas that the made-up group was plotting against Donald Trump, who they said was trying to take down the group. With the help of QAnon, new theories about Pizza-Gate spread to platforms like TikTok. This time, those targeted by the lies included celebrities and well-known businesspeople, in addition to politicians.

Online Bullying Can End in Tragedy

Suicide can be one tragic result of a cyber mob attack. Often, cyber mobs will encourage a victim to take their own life. Hearing this message multiple times from multiple people—even strangers who do not know anything about them—can lead a victim to take or attempt to take their life in order to escape the abuse.

Brandy Vela was a senior in high school when she took her own life after years of bullying, both online and offline. She had been harassed about her weight for years at school. By 2016, the harassment had moved online. Bullies created a fake Facebook profile for her and used the account to send sexual messages to other people. They even posted her real telephone number so men would call about the sexual offers. Other trolls would call or text late at night. They talked about her weight and about her physical features. When Vela reported a cyberbullying page, Facebook would take it down, but within days, another would be started.

Alice Marwick is an expert on disinformation at the University of North Carolina at Chapel Hill. She said, "PizzaGate never went away because it encompasses very potent forces."[3] People care a lot about the safety of children and have strong opinions about powerful people abusing their power. This is part of the reason why so many people believe the false ideas behind PizzaGate and QAnon and use them to continue to harass innocent people online.

Some victims of cyber mobs have actually done something society sees as wrong. In these cases, cyber mobs form as a way of shaming them. Shaming happens in groups as a way to keep the social norms, or unwritten rules of society. Online shaming can sometimes seem like a normal or funny thing. For example, some men who sit on public transportation take up a lot of room by sitting with their legs spread open, pushing into other people's seating areas. When someone sees a man do this in public, they might take his picture, share it online, and complain about how the man is taking up too much space. They do this to try to enforce the social norm of not invading other people's personal space. The man whose picture was shared may never find out, but this kind of shaming works for anyone who sees it. By

pillory

stock

Public shaming is nothing new. Pillories and stocks were used to publicly shame people believed to have committed crimes. They weren't completely outlawed in all parts of the United States until 1905.

seeing the anonymous man be shamed, others understand that the punishment for breaking this social norm might be that others laugh at them online. This kind of fear often makes people keep social norms in place. However, when a cyber mob forms, the shaming is generally far harsher than it should be. Trolls and cyber mobs violate social norms online by being cruel, but they feel it is okay because they have convinced themselves their target deserves it.

Responding to Hate

Many victims of cyber mobs stop going online. More specifically, many stop using social media. For some, this is temporary, but for others, it is a permanent choice. Other victims, however, feel the need to stay on these platforms to stand up for themselves and correct the false information being spread about them by the cyber mobs. Every situation is different, and there is not always a clear right or wrong way to handle being a victim of lies online. Sometimes, correcting the cyber mob will make the harassment worse. Other times, victims feel things will only get worse if they leave the conversation.

When victims of cyber mobs leave social media, they lose the ability to participate in many aspects of the world. They may lose touch with friends who don't live nearby, miss out on job and social opportunities, or lose sight of what is happening in the world. Additionally, if a person fears being a target of a cyber mob, they may be scared to speak their true feelings. They may choose to keep their ideas suppressed. When voices are silenced by cyber mobs, the debate stops, and the truth can be hidden. This censorship of ideas hurts everyone.

No matter how an individual decides to respond to it, online harassment is serious and should be reported to a trusted adult. The adult can help determine the severity of the issue and report it to higher authorities if necessary. Even if the harassment does not appear to break any laws or seem that serious to an outsider, the victim may be in need of real help. They may be dealing with serious depression or other mental health issues stemming from the harassment. They could also be in physical danger if a troll decides to take their hate from the internet to the offline world. Online threats should always be taken seriously.

Your Opinion Matters!

1. Do you think the mob responding to the man who killed Cecil the lion was doing a good or bad thing?

2. Have you ever seen a post online and shared it without checking to make sure it was true?

3. If you were a victim of widespread lies online, do you think you would engage with the cyber mob and tell them why they are wrong or try to ignore them?

HARASSMENT OF GROUPS

According to a 2020 study by the Pew Research Center, 55 percent of people think online harassment is a major problem. In 2017, the Center had found that 41 percent of Americans personally experienced online harassment in some way. In the 2020 study, this statistic was the same. However, while the rate of people experiencing online harassment did not change, the specific types of harassment they were subjected to did—and they had gotten more serious. In the three years between the two studies, reported instances of physical threats, sexual harassment, and stalking increased significantly. People in the 2020 study were also more likely to report being harassed in multiple ways than those in the 2017 study.

Of those in the 2020 study who said they were targeted by online harassment, half said they had been harassed because of their political views. While politics has always been a hot-button issue for disagreement, Emily Vogels, a research associate at the Pew Research Center, points to a growing rate of disagreement and dislike between people with opposing political viewpoints to help explain this statistic.

When someone is harassed online, it is often out there for others to see right away. It can be difficult to decide whether to defend yourself and get into an argument or try to ignore the harasser.

Cyber Attacks in Sports

Female athletes are common targets of online harassment, often about their appearance, sexuality, and femininity. Male athletes get harassed too, but harassment aimed at them is more commonly related to their athletic performance.

Like all celebrities, athletes can fall victim to hacking. In 2016, a group called Fancy Bear illegally hacked the World Anti-Doping Agency's database. The agency works to monitor and promote the fight against the use of banned substances in sports. The database contained private medical information about athletes from the 2016 Olympics. The hackers publicly posted information they claimed to be from the database about several American athletes, including gymnast Simone Biles and tennis players Venus and Serena Williams.

Fancy Bear claimed the documents showed the athletes had used banned substances; however, according to the U.S. Anti-Doping Agency (USADA), the athletes were only using needed medication and had followed the rules. For example, the hackers said Biles tested positive for methylphenidate, commonly known as Ritalin, a drug used to treat attention-deficit/hyperactivity disorder (ADHD).

"I have ADHD and have taken medicine for it since I was a kid," Biles explained on Twitter. "Please know, I believe in clean sport, have always followed the rules, and will continue to do so as fair play is critical to sport and is very important to me."[1]

The head of the USADA, Travis Tygart, also responded to the hack. He said:

It's unthinkable that in the Olympic movement, hackers would illegally obtain confidential medical information in an attempt to smear athletes to make it look as if they have done something wrong. The athletes haven't. In fact, in each of the situations, the athlete has done everything right in adhering to the global rules for obtaining permission to use a needed medication.[2]

1. Quoted in Josh Meyer, "Russian Hackers Post 'Medical Files' of Simone Biles, Serena Williams," NBC News, September 13, 2016, www.nbcnews.com/storyline/2016-rio-summer-olympics/russian-hackers-post-medical-files-biles-serena-williams-n647571.

2. Quoted in Meyer, "Russian Hackers Post 'Medical Files' of Simone Biles, Serena Williams."

Simone Biles

However, Vogels also said, "Bear in mind that politics isn't the only perceived reason for harassment being on the rise. Over the past several years, rising shares of online harassment targets have said they think they were harassed because of their gender, race, ethnicity, religion or sexual orientation."[1]

To Vogels' point, in the 2020 study, 33 percent of those harassed online said they had been harassed because of their gender, 29 percent said they had been harassed because of their race or ethnicity, 19 percent said they had been harassed because of their religion, and 16 percent said they had been harassed because of their sexual orientation. Many times, victims of cyber mobs are harassed for more than one of these reasons.

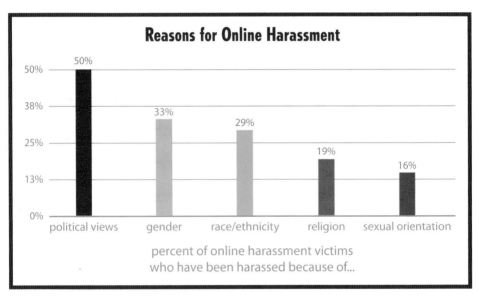

Of people who have been harassed online, this chart shows how many say they have been harassed for each of the stated reasons. Some people were harassed for more than one of these reasons.

Common Targets

Women, members of the LGBTQ+ community, people with disabilities or special needs, religious minorities, and people of

In-Person Attacks and the Internet

Today, the internet even has a lot to do with in-person attacks. In 2016, there was a shooting at Pulse nightclub in Orlando, Florida. Pulse was a well-known gay nightclub where many members of the LGBTQ+ community in Orlando went to have fun. Sadly, on June 12, 2016, a gunman killed 49 people at the club and wounded many others. At the time, this was the deadliest mass shooting in the history of the United States. The shooter, Omar Mateen, posted terrorism-related content on Facebook before the attack. He also used Facebook to search for such content. He was even said to have been using Facebook on his phone during parts of the attack.

Facebook and Twitter were also used to warn people to stay away from the area during the attack, and for the first time in the United States, Facebook turned on their "Safety Check" feature. This allows people to mark themselves safe from a tragic event so their friends and family far away can know they're OK. Some survivors of the shooting also posted about their experiences of the attack online.

After the Pulse nightclub shooting, people all around the world gathered to remember the victims and fight for change. Activists are shown here at a vigil in Kolkata, India.

color are frequent targets of online harassment. Many times, victims of cyber mobs fall into more than one of these categories. When a person or group of people says cruel things about another group of people based on their gender, race, ethnicity, religion, sexual orientation, or physical and mental abilities, this can be termed hate speech. Hate speech online can turn into hate crimes. Even if violence does not happen, being the target of a cyber mob can cause pain and fear.

Amnesty International's Troll Patrol project studied millions of tweets that were sent to 778 women journalists and politicians in 2017. Those included in the study were from the United States and the United Kingdom and represented different races and ethnicities, as well as different parts of the political spectrum. The study found that 7.1 percent of the tweets sent to the women were "problematic" or "abusive." Women of color, however, were 34 percent more likely to be the targets of these kinds of tweets than white women. Specifically, a report on the study stated, "Black women were disproportionately targeted, being 84% more likely than white women to be mentioned in abusive or problematic tweets."[2]

Members of the LGBTQ+ community (which includes people who identify as lesbian, gay, bisexual, transgender, queer, or questioning, among other sexual orientations and gender identities) are often targets of cyber mobs too. LGBTQ+ people are often targeted for hate speech and hate crimes. Although there has been more acceptance of LGBTQ+ people in recent years, they are still likely to be harassed online for their sexuality or gender identity.

After the terrorist attacks of September 11, 2001, many Muslims were targeted for harassment, as they still are today. With the rise of the internet, much of the harassment has moved online. Threats to Muslims often center on false ideas about their religious beliefs. Muslim women who post pictures of themselves wearing a traditional hair and neck covering, called a hijab, are often flooded with messages from anonymous accounts that focus not only on their religion but also on their gender. One Muslim woman on Twitter received more than 100 death and rape threats within an hour of a cyber mob forming to harass her.

Jewish people have also long been targets of abuse, and in the digital age, many have become targets of cyber mobs. During the 2016 U.S. presidential election, anti-Semites (people who hate Jewish people) created a cyber mob to attack Jewish journalists. The anti-Semitic cyber mob would identify a Jewish reporter and then begin to harass them on Twitter. When a Jewish reporter for *Newsweek*, Kurt Eichenwald, wrote about the harassment he received, the threats began to target his family and children. Eichenwald, who has epilepsy—a disorder that causes seizures—received a video from the cyber mob that had strobing lights, which are known to cause seizures in people with epilepsy. Luckily, Eichenwald was able to drop his computer before the video caused a seizure. However, in December 2016, Eichenwald received another video intended to give him an epileptic seizure. This time, it worked. Eichenwald and his wife filed a police report, and the suspect was arrested on multiple federal charges, including cyberstalking.

After the 2020 presidential election, Donald Trump attempted to have the election results overturned in several states where he lost. Without any evidence to support his claims, he said the election had been rigged against him. One of the states where he challenged the results was Wisconsin. After the Wisconsin Supreme Court rejected Trump's lawsuit attempting to overturn the state's election results, several members of the court became victims of online threats, including Justices Jill Karofsky and Rebecca Dallet, who were both targets of anti-Semitic attacks. Wisconsin Supreme Court Chief Justice Patience Roggensack responded to the attacks:

> *I acknowledge that all members of the public have the constitutional right to speak in criticism of public servants, which certainly includes all justices on the Wisconsin Supreme Court.*

While Donald Trump may not have directly told his followers to form a cyber mob, some people believe his repeated false claims that the election was rigged encouraged them to do so.

However, no justice should be threatened or intimidated based on his or her religious beliefs.[3]

#GamerGate

In 2014, women working in the gaming industry were targeted by a cyber mob. The harassment started when a game designer, Zoë Quinn, created a text-based game called *Depression Quest*. Many gamers claimed they were harassing Quinn because they disliked the game, but most outside observers said the true reason was likely because Quinn was a woman. Chat logs released from 4chan showed that some members of the cyber mob were making comments about how they did not care about *Depression Quest*, they just wanted to destroy Quinn's life and get her to die by suicide.

The harassment escalated after Quinn's ex-boyfriend wrote online that she had cheated on him with several other men. Since one of the men briefly mentioned *Depression Quest* in an article he had written, the cyber mob decided Quinn had done this to get a good review for *Depression Quest*. They began sending her death threats and started using the hashtag #GamerGate on social media. The man spoke out to say that he had written the article before being with Quinn and noted that he did not review the game, he simply mentioned that it existed. None of this mattered to the mob; Quinn was doxed and had to leave her home to protect her safety.

Eventually, #GamerGate spread from targeting Quinn to targeting any women who spoke up about sexism in the gaming industry. Some women were targeted simply for criticizing #GamerGate. Brianna Wu, the owner of a gaming company, began receiving online threats after she tweeted about #GamerGate in a joking manner. She, too, left her home and work and went into hiding. Gamer and actress Felicia Day was doxed just minutes after posting online that she was afraid to talk about #GamerGate for fear of retaliation. Members of the cyber mob denied that they were targeting women simply for being women,

Zoë Quinn responded to #GamerGate by fighting back against the cyber mob. She co-founded an online group called Crash Override, which helps other victims of cyber harassment.

but former professional football player Chris Kluwe pointed out that he and other men were not doxed for criticizing the cyber mob. #GamerGate ended up proving many of the things women in the industry had complained about.

When Private Photos Become Public

The internet has become a large part of socializing, but this also makes people vulnerable to cyber harassment on social media, through text messaging, and through video games. One way many people are targeted is by someone sharing their personal photos. Sometimes, couples send explicit photos to each other. Adults should never be exchanging these types of photos with minors. If they do, it should be reported to a trusted adult immediately. Even if both people are minors and willingly participating, those under 18 can be charged with producing or possessing child pornography. Additionally, people must remember that the person they are sending the photo to will always have it unless they choose to delete it. Even on apps such as Snapchat, where the photo disappears after a short amount of time, someone can take a screenshot. The app lets people know when someone takes a screenshot, but this does not help the person get the picture back.

When a couple breaks up, some people may share explicit photos of their ex to get back at them for ending the relationship. Some websites post photos of unwilling victims—mostly young women—to shame them. Sometimes, they charge the women a fee to take the photos down, which is known as extortion—an illegal practice where someone gains money through threats or violence. However, by the time victims find out they are on these websites, the images are often spread across the internet and almost impossible to remove completely.

According to the Cyber Civil Rights Initiative (CCRI):

The term "revenge porn," though frequently used, is somewhat misleading. Many perpetrators are not motivated by revenge or by any personal feelings toward the victim. A more accurate term is nonconsensual pornography (NCP), defined as the distribution of sexually graphic images of individuals without their consent.[4]

The CCRI has a helpful website that explains how to delete nonconsensual images on all the major social media websites. Steps include documenting the post, unfriending or disconnecting from the person who posted the photo, and reporting it to the social media company and law enforcement. Many states have laws against NCP, and the CCRI offers resources to help understand what these laws are in different states.

Celebrities and Cyber Mobs

Famous people are often targeted by cyber mobs. Celebrities, especially female ones, are often the targets of hacking campaigns that steal personal photographs in an effort to embarrass them or damage their reputation. In 2014, members of 4chan broke into the online documents of a number of female celebrities. The hackers were able to steal the women's explicit photos and then spread them to other websites, including Twitter. Actress Jennifer Lawrence was one of the women affected. Lawrence told *Vanity Fair* magazine, "I was just so afraid. I didn't know how this would affect my career."[5] Lawrence and other celebrities affected by the theft worked with the Federal Bureau of Investigation (FBI) to try to recover the stolen photos and punish the thieves.

Many celebrities have social media accounts where they can interact with fans and talk about issues that are important to them. This openness and connectivity can make them easy targets for hatred. Some have chosen to shut down their social media or put their internet use on hold until cyber mobs choose a different target. In 2018, Kelly Marie Tran, who made history as the first woman of color to star in a *Star Wars* movie when she played Rose Tico, made the decision to quit social media. After appearing in the famous franchise, Tran

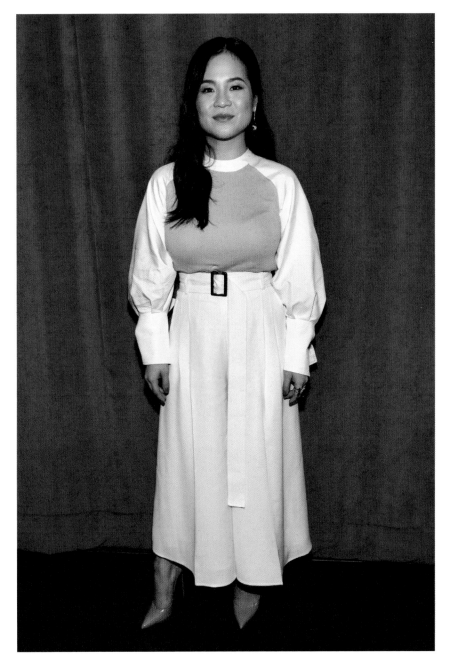

Some people fear they will miss out on things if they leave social media. However, Tran doesn't regret her choice. In 2020, she told *Entertainment Tonight* that the decision was what was best for her.

became the victim of online harassment. The abuse was racist and sexist in nature, often directed at the fact that she is an Asian (specifically, Southeast Asian) American woman.

After her departure from social media, Tran discussed her decision in an article she wrote for the *New York Times*. She began:

> *It wasn't their words, it's that I started to believe them.*
>
> *Their words seemed to confirm what growing up as a woman and a person of color already taught me: that I belonged in margins and spaces, valid only as a minor character in their lives and stories.*[6]

Later in the article, she wrote:

> *I want to live in a world where children of color don't spend their entire adolescence wishing to be white. I want to live in a world where women are not subjected to scrutiny for their appearance, or their actions, or their general existence. I want to live in a world where people of all races, religions, socioeconomic classes, sexual orientations, gender identities and abilities are seen as what they have always been: human beings.*[7]

Celebrities aren't always just victims of cyber mobs. Sometimes they encourage them. Celebrities with large and dedicated fan bases have a lot of influence. They may not do it on purpose, but if they say something negative about someone, it might lead their fans to troll the person. In 2018, actress Hilary Duff took to Instagram to complain about a neighbor she said was disturbing her and her family. She said this neighbor was loud, left trash around, and smoked so much that her own apartment smelled from it. This certainly sounds like inconsiderate behavior, but some people thought Duff crossed a line when she posted the neighbor's name and a screenshot of his Instagram account. Some of Duff's fans started reposting the content on their pages.

The neighbor claims that he even received threats from some of Duff's fans. While Duff did not specifically ask her fans to do this, some would argue that by posting the neighbor's name and Instagram account, a reasonable person could have assumed such an outcome might occur.

Your Opinion Matters!

1. Why do you think people online got harassed for their political views more often in 2020 than they did in 2017?

2. Why are certain people more likely to be targets of cyber mobs than others?

3. Do you think it is OK for a celebrity to identify someone online that they have a personal disagreement or problem with?

Username:

Username

Password

STANDING UP TO CYBER ABUSE

It's important to protect personal information online. Strong passwords and privacy settings can help. Still, cyber mobs can be difficult to fight against. While cyber mobs and trolls are the ones who should be held responsible for their attacks, it's still a good idea to think before you post anything that could be seen as controversial. Unfortunately, laws haven't fully caught up to the internet, and it can still sometimes be difficult to get justice for victims of online harassment.

Protect Your Information

Protecting information online can be difficult, but it is important for keeping power out of the hands of cyber mobs. Experts recommend creating a different difficult password for every account and using more than one email address. There are programs that will come up with hard-to-hack passwords for you. The password will be a string of seemingly random letters, numbers, and other characters that would be hard for someone to guess. The program will remember these passwords for you, so you don't have to memorize them. You just have to remember the password for the program. These programs, as well as other websites that contain sensitive

◀ Always using the same password might make it easy to remember, but it also makes it easy for hackers to get into all your accounts. There are apps to help you remember your passwords.

information, may require two-factor authentication. This means you need to confirm it's you with a second method, in addition to your password. When someone signs into the account, the website may send a special code to a cell phone or email address on record. You then have to enter the code before the program or website logs you in. Having to take this second step to sign in prevents someone without access to both the password and the cell phone or email address from logging in. Additionally, most new cell phones today have special security settings, such as fingerprint and facial authentication. This can make it harder for a person who has somehow gained access to another person's phone to get into it and find their personal information or photos.

Privacy settings allow social media accounts to be restricted so that only friends can view the content. This helps limit the ways a cyber mob can reach someone. Even with serious privacy restrictions, though, it is always a good idea to keep some personal information off a profile, such as address, phone number, workplace, or school.

If someone does become the victim of a cyber attack, they should document their abusers' posts. When harassing accounts are blocked online by a victim, the past harassment can often no longer be seen by the victim. This can be both good and bad. People being harassed do not want to see the cruel messages again, but having proof of a cyber mob attack is important. If a victim goes to the police to report the harassment, it is important to have a copy of the messages.

Comebacks and Counterspeech

Groups that are normally the targets of cyber mobs and cyberbullying have been effective in promoting counterspeech. Counterspeech means using words that challenge the messages of hatred by presenting counterarguments, facts, or even calling out the hatred for what it is. Counterspeech can be when people use the words of the cyber mob against it through either parody or elevation to the attention of others. By bringing the cyber mob to the attention of the wider public, counterspeech can show victims that they are not alone and that the cyber mob's views are not socially accepted.

The Dangerous Speech Project studies speech, including things expressed online, that inspires or encourages violence between groups of people. Cathy Buerger, the group's director of research, talked about effective methods of counterspeech at a conference in 2019. She said one of her favorite methods is done by #Jagärhär, a Swedish group that works together to respond to negative and hateful posts in the comment sections of news articles on Facebook.

"On the #Jagärhär Facebook page, group administrators post links to articles with hateful comments, directing their members to counterspeak there," Buerger said. "Members tag their posts with #Jagärhär (which means, "I am here"), so that other members can find their posts and like them."[1]

News outlets commonly rank their comments by relevance. Facebook determines relevance by looking at how many likes and replies a comment gets. By liking the counterspeech comments, members of #Jagärhär drive them up in relevance ranking. This moves the counterspeech comments up to the top of the comments section. The goal is to make it less likely that people will see hateful comments—and according to Buerger, it often works.

Another form of counterspeech occurred in the world of sports media. Women in this field often receive cruel and harassing tweets and other online messages. In 2016, men who run a podcast called *Just Not Sports* produced a video called "#MoreThanMean." In the video, everyday men read mean tweets that female sports reporters received. They read the tweets sitting face to face with the woman who originally received the abuse. In the video, the tweets started out with mild insults but quickly turned into rape and death threats. The men could not look at the women anymore and asked if they were required to read the tweets out loud. By reading the harassment while looking at the victim, the men were able to understand the effect cyber harassment has on a real person. The words that normally lose meaning on a computer screen had come to life, and the men—as well as those watching the video—could begin to understand the real consequences that online abuse can inflict on someone.

Counterspeech does not return hate with hate or try to personally attack members of a cyber mob. When this happens, those responding turn into trolls themselves. Instead, counterspeech works to change the conversation by providing support for victims, showing respect for everyone involved, and challenging ideas that are hurtful. Counterspeech may not be able to directly prove statements incorrect, but it can work to show everyone involved that civility and mutual respect are important parts of any discussion.

By using counter-hacking and other research, trolls' real names can be identified. Some victims have started finding a troll's real name and then researching to find someone in their life who might hold them accountable. Victims will send these people a screenshot of the online content written by a troll. Trolls may then face many of the same consequences as the victim of a cyber mob. They could lose jobs, be suspended in school, or be in trouble with parents or partners. However, some people feel this kind of behavior is no better than what the trolls do.

A Guide for Good Behavior?

Some people believe the entire internet needs a code of conduct. The Internet Society, a non-profit organization that aims to keep the internet safe and open for everyone, has written one for its members. It includes making sure work done on the internet does not hurt anyone. The code also talks about how to keep the internet open to everyone by not making technology that keeps people away. The most important part of the code

Is Shaming Helpful?

Researcher Dr. Brené Brown believes shaming someone might actually make their behavior worse:

Based on my research and the research of other shame researchers, I believe that there is a profound difference between shame and guilt. I believe that guilt is adaptive and helpful—it's holding something we've done or failed to do up against our values and feeling psychological discomfort.

I define shame as the intensely painful feeling or experience of believing that we are flawed and therefore unworthy of love and belonging—something we've experienced, done, or failed to do makes us unworthy of connection.

I don't believe shame is helpful or productive. In fact, I think shame is much more likely to be the source of destructive, hurtful behavior than the solution or cure. I think the fear of disconnection can make us dangerous.[1]

To fight online bullies, counterspeech and other measures should focus on creating a feeling of guilt in the abusers, rather than shaming them. Helping cyberbullies understand why their behavior is wrong may help them overcome the need to be cruel. Instead of feeling ashamed as a person, they can take responsibility for their behaviors and make changes.

1. Brené Brown, "Shame v. Guilt," Brené Brown, January 14, 2013, brenebrown. com/2013/01/14/2013114shame-v-guilt-html/.

asks that everyone follow the norms of internet etiquette, or what most people consider an acceptable way to behave. For instance, it is considered a violation of etiquette to post unkind things about someone online. A universal code of ethics could remind everyone that even online, other people have rights and deserve respect.

A code of conduct or ethics could help protect internet speech. It could also help make the internet a better place. By reminding everyone of their rights and responsibilities, these kinds of codes might change the way people act online.

Finding Help

There are many organizations that support victims of cyber mobs and online harassment in general. These groups put together websites, books, and apps to help people deal with cyber abuse. There are also apps that help people report and stop cyberbullying. One of these apps is called STOPit. STOPit lets any user take a picture of cyber harassment and anonymously send the picture to someone who can help. Many STOPit users are children or teens. They can report cyberbullying directly to their parents or school so an adult can step in and help.

In most schools, teachers have some sort of training to look for bullying among their students, but they are not always aware of what is happening online. Additionally, schools cannot monitor the private emails or the social media accounts of their students. However, they can see anything that is made public. Some schools have started looking at public social media profiles for evidence of bullying, but this has led to controversy as people argue that the school should not be able to punish students for posts that are made outside of school. Many people are unsure of how much power schools should have over students, especially when it comes to things that are posted online. This is a subject that is likely to be debated for some time.

Most parents want to know if their child is being bullied. They want to be able to help the child deal with it, but many parents do not know all the ways kids can be bullied. They may not even know the names of some social media websites or apps. This can make it hard to understand the problem when their children report bullying. One U.S. government agency is trying to change that. The Substance Abuse and Mental Health Services

Administration (SAMHSA) created an app just for parents called KnowBullying. Parents can download the app and learn about bullying and the internet. This kind of education can help parents support kids who are being bullied online or in school. According to SAMHSA, "Research shows that parents and caregivers who spend at least 15 minutes a day talking with their children or teens help build strong relationships, and prevent bullying."[2]

Another government resource is the website StopBullying.gov. This website, run by the U.S. Department of Health and Human Services, has resources for parents, children, and even teachers to help stop all types of bullying, including cyberbullying.

The Future of Online Abuse

While cyber mobs have increased in recent years, so have the ways they can be stopped. People working against cyber mobs are developing new technology every day to help keep the internet a safe place to share ideas. Lawyers and police officers are working together with community groups to learn current laws and create new laws to prosecute leaders and members of cyber mobs. In the fight against cyber mobs, everyone online has a part to play. Every day, people online are becoming more aware of digital citizenship and the power of helping each other fight hate.

Many websites give users the ability to report abuse when they see it. Additionally, some websites have workers or volunteers who make sure the policies of the website, especially regarding cruel or offensive speech, are not broken. These people are referred to as moderators, or mods. Some may be more strict in their interpretation of the policies than others. Other websites use artificial intelligence, or AI, instead of real people. AI uses algorithms to act like humans would online. These AI programs can be bots (short for robots), scripts, or other software that steps in to identify and delete abusive posts. However, whenever AI is involved, there is always some debate. Many people believe AI should not be able to automatically delete things, otherwise the

Laws and Education

There are many current laws that could be used to stop cyber mobs and their harassment tactics, but these can only be enforced if the harassers can be identified. Since many people hide their identity online, this can be difficult. Additionally, the American legal system is often difficult for people to figure out, and legal fees tend to be expensive. To some people, it is not worth the time, effort, and money it takes to bring a lawsuit against someone. However, for others, the harassment is so harmful that they need to take action. Lawmakers are currently looking at ways to change existing laws so they can better protect people from online harassment.

There is also a great need for more lawyers and police officers to be trained in how to respond to online hate and cyber mobs. Some advocacy groups have developed courses for police and legal advocates. For instance, the Tyler Clementi Foundation was founded by the family of Tyler Clementi, an 18-year-old college student who ended his life after becoming a victim of cyber harassment. The foundation trains lawyers on how to represent victims of cyberbullying and uses research to educate judges, lawmakers, and the public about cyber mobs.

Other groups work with police officers and communities to learn the signs of cyberbullying and the best ways to help a

potential for censorship is too great. They feel a real person still needs to review the things these programs flag and unflag them if they are not cruel or harmful. Balancing moderation and free speech is a tricky thing, and even humans still have trouble with it. Robots are not advanced enough yet to do it on their own.

Can We Make a Change?

Laws about online abuse differ all over the United States and the world. Many of these laws need to be updated or better enforced, but, especially in recent years, many of them have been effective.

victim. Victims of cyber mobs can feel alone when a mob is attacking. If they decide to reach out to a school counselor, teacher, or police officer, these helpers need to know how to respond.

Adults who work in certain fields, such as police officers, sometimes take special training classes to learn how best to help victims of online harassment.

However, while laws are important to protect people, some individuals do not have a problem with breaking the law. To make the internet a better, safer place for everyone, people must work on changing trolls' and cyber mobs' attitudes. This can be difficult to do, and there is no one single way that works for everyone; however, social experts have proposed several ideas. Sometimes, ignoring the hateful messages is the best way to deal with them, but other times, as several victims have found, confronting the cyber mob may help stop the abuse. This is because when people see the effect their words have on others, it might stop them from harassing people. However, this tactic does not work on people whose intention is to cause others harm.

With the help of the internet, people are able to participate in global conversations. Just like people have citizenship in their countries, people on the internet have digital citizenship. With this citizenship comes a responsibility to keep the conversation open to everyone.

Digital citizenship means knowing how to use the internet effectively, appropriately, and responsibly. It means knowing the consequences of online speech and helping the community report cyber mobs. Learning about the ways that cyber mobs hurt people is important because knowledge helps good people recognize bad behavior and know how to act. Counterspeech and other tools for helping victims of cyber attacks can be learned with the help of online communities.

It is up to the people who use the internet to report hate when they see it. When hate is reported and counterspeech is practiced regularly, the internet becomes safer for everyone. Right now, people often feel they can say whatever they want online without consequences. A community of active digital citizens can change that. They can make it the norm to be kind and stand up for others. Being a good digital citizen also means taking responsibility for privacy. This involves not sharing other people's photos or information without their consent. Only the owner of the photos or information can provide this consent.

Good digital citizens learn the rules of good behavior on the internet. They do not use anonymity to hurt other people. If a good digital citizen sees other people bullying, they do not join the cyber mob. They learn to recognize when their own words are hurtful. They think before they type. Good digital citizens know that just because something can be done does not always mean it should be done. The internet has rules of civility just like regular society. Good digital citizens know these rules and follow them.

When other people stand up for a victim, they may be able to change the course of a cyber mob. However, fighting back with mean words only gives permission for the attacker to keep being mean. When a cyber mob attacks, sometimes the best way to fight is to remain calm and kind.

How Can You Help?

If you see online bullying or harassment happening, don't just stand by and watch. Be an upstander—someone who takes action to stop bullying when they see it happening. If someone you know is being harassed online and you feel comfortable

Sometimes, just knowing they have a friend or person to talk to can help a victim of a cyber mob. It's not directly ending the harassment, but it can still make the victim feel better.

doing so, you can reach out to them privately to let them know they are not alone and offer your support. Being a friend to victims of cyber mobs is a simple way to help make the internet a better place.

You might not always feel comfortable reaching out to the victim, and that is OK. Additionally, it's not always safe to step in directly to defend a victim of a cyber mob. There are still ways you can help, though. If the website or app has a way to report harassment, doing so can be helpful. It may prompt the website to remove the harmful content and the users behind it. However, we know this doesn't always solve the problem. Reporting the harassment to a trusted adult, such as a parent or teacher, is often the best way for children and teens to handle these situations. Adults have ways to hold the trolls and cyber mobs accountable and can help find support for the victim.

Most importantly, don't become a troll or part of a cyber mob yourself. Think before you post. At first, it might seem harmless to repost or share a funny post or picture you see. However, could doing so hurt someone? Could it spread misinformation? Remember, trolls don't always set out to be trolls. Sometimes it happens accidentally. Other times, people who were initially victims become bullies themselves as a response to the hate they received. When using the internet, it's best to spread kindness, not hate.

Your Opinion Matters!

1. How can counterspeech show victims they're not alone?

2. Do you think there should be an overarching code of conduct for the internet?

3. What's involved in being a good digital citizen?

The following are some suggestions for taking what you've just read and applying that information to your everyday life.

- If you see harassment online, report it to the website or an adult you feel safe communicating about it with.

- Before you share any news online, be sure to do your own research to confirm that it is true and sharing it would not spread misinformation.

- Think about memes before sharing them. If it could be hurtful to the person or people in them, don't share them.

- Don't post your personal information—or anyone else's—online.

- Use secure privacy settings on any online profiles you have.

- If someone you know and feel comfortable talking to is being harassed, let them know you are there for them.

Introduction: Socializing Safely

1. Engrossed Bill of Rights, September 25, 1789; General Records of the United States Government; Record Group 11; National Archives.

Chapter One: When the Internet Turns Negative

1. Quoted in Ben Dattner Ph.D., "Preventing 'Groupthink'," *Psychology Today*, April 20, 2011, www.psychologytoday.com/us/blog/credit-and-blame-work/201104/preventing-groupthink.

2. Irving L. Janis, "Groupthink in Washington," *New York Times*, May 28, 1973. p. 15, www.nytimes.com/1973/05/28/archives/groupthink-in-washington.html.

3. Joe Dawson, "Who Is That? The Study of Anonymity and Behavior," *Observer*, Association for Psychological Science, vol. 31, no. 4, April 2018, pp. 15–17, www.psychologicalscience.org/redesign/wp-content/uploads/2018/03/April_OBS_2018_3-30pdf-reduced.pdf.

4. *McIntyre v. Ohio Elections Commission*, 514 U.S. 334 (1995). www.law.cornell.edu/supct/html/93-986.ZO.html.

5. "United Nations Strategy and Plan of Action on Hate Speech," United Nations, May 2019, www.un.org/en/genocideprevention/documents/UN%20Strategy%20and%20Plan%20of%20Action%20on%20Hate%20Speech%2018%20June%20SYNOPSIS.pdf. p. 2 (accessed January 26, 2021).

6. Ellen Pao, "The Trolls Are Winning the Battle for the Internet," *Washington Post*, July 16, 2015, www.washingtonpost.com/opinions/we-cannot-let-the-internet-trolls-win/2015/07/16/91b1a2d2-2b17-11e5-bd33-395c05608059_story.html.

Chapter Two: Many Methods of Harassment

1. Quoted in Trilby Beresford, "Help Prevent Bullying with Ross Ellis, Founder of STOMP Out Bullying," Amy Poehler's Smart Girls, November 16, 2016, amysmartgirls.com/help-prevent-bullying-with-ross-ellis-founder-of-stomp-out-bullying-d2797db0be33#.vl1pgiv35.

2. Quoted in Natalie Wolchover, "Why Is Everyone on the Internet So Angry?" *Scientific American*, July 25, 2012, www.scientificamerican.com/article/why-is-everyone-on-the-Internet-so-angry/.

3. Quoted in Wolchover, "Why Is Everyone on the Internet So Angry?"

4. Quoted in Scottie Andrew and Kat Jennings, "Parents on TikTok mock people with disabilities for the 'New Teacher Challenge.' These women are reclaiming their images," CNN, August 30, 2020, www.cnn.com/2020/08/30/us/tiktok-new-teacher-challenge-bullying-trnd/index.html.

5. "Hogg on Ingraham: 'A bully is a bully,'" CNN, www.cnn.com/videos/us/2018/03/31/david-hogg-ingraham-bully-bts-nr.cnn (accessed January 26, 2021).

Chapter Three: Online Actions, Real Consequences

1. Kenneth Westhues, "At the Mercy of the Mob," *OHS Canada*, vol. 18, no. 8, December 2002, pp. 30–36, www.kwesthues.com/ohs-canada.htm.

2. *Rosenblatt v. Baer*, 383 U.S. 75, 86 (1966).

3. Quoted in Cecilia Kang and Sheera Frenkel, "'PizzaGate' Conspiracy Theory Thrives Anew in the TikTok Era," *New York Times*, June 27, 2020, www.nytimes.com/2020/06/27/technology/pizzagate-justin-bieber-qanon-tiktok.html.

Chapter Four: Harassment of Groups

1. Quoted in Drew Desilver, "Q&A: What We've Learned about Online Harassment," *Fact Tank: News in the Numbers*, Pew Research Center, January 13, 2021, www.pewresearch.org/fact-tank/2021/01/13/qa-what-weve-learned-about-online-harassment/.

2. "Troll Patrol Findings," Amnesty International, decoders.amnesty.org/projects/troll-patrol/findings (accessed January 26, 2021).

3. Statement of Chief Justice Patience Drake Roggensack, Wisconsin Supreme Court (Madison, WI: December 25, 2020), www.wicourts.gov/news/view.jsp?id=1297.

4. "What is 'Revenge Porn'?" Cyber Civil Rights Initiative, www.cybercivilrights.org (accessed January 26, 2021).

5. Quoted in Sam Kashner, "Both Huntress and Prey," *Vanity Fair*, November 2014, www.vanityfair.com/hollywood/2014/10/jennifer-lawrence-photo-hacking-privacy.

6. Kelly Marie Tran, "I Won't Be Marginalized by Online Harassment," *New York Times*, August 21, 2018, www.nytimes.com/2018/08/21/movies/kelly-marie-tran.html.

7. Tran, "I Won't Be Marginalized by Online Harassment."

Chapter Five: Standing Up to Cyber Abuse

1. Quoted in Daniel Jones and Susan Benesch, "Combating Hate Speech Through Counterspeech," Berkman Klein Center for Internet & Society at Harvard University, August 9, 2019, cyber.harvard.edu/story/2019-08/combating-hate-speech-through-counterspeech.

2. Substance Abuse and Mental Health Services Administration, "KnowBullying Mobile App," July 2014, store.samhsa.gov/product/knowbullying.

FOR MORE INFORMATION

Books: Nonfiction

Glaser, Pam T., and Judy Monroe Peterson. *Shutting Down Cyberbullies*. New York, NY: Rosen Publishing, 2020.

Mapua, Jeff. *Coping with Cyberbullying*. New York, NY: Rosen Publishing, 2018.

New York Times Editorial Staff. *Cyberbullying: A Deadly Trend*. New York, NY: New York Times Educational Publishing, 2019.

Books: Fiction

Averbuch, Sheila M. *Friend Me*. New York, NY: Scholastic Press, 2020.

Cooner, Donna. *Screenshot*. New York, NY: Point, 2018.

Farizan, Sara. *Here to Stay*. Chapel Hill, NC: Algonquin, 2019.

Littman, Sarah Darer. *Backlash*. New York, NY: Scholastic Press, 2015.

Websites

eTAG
www.endtechabuse.org/
eTag, or End Tech Abuse Across Generations, is a project that is part of the California Coalition Against Sexual Assault. The website offers resources and information about the use of technology in cases of sexual assault, domestic violence, dating violence, and stalking (including cyberstalking).

PEN America: Online Harassment Field Manual
onlineharassmentfieldmanual.pen.org/
This online manual offers useful tools, tips, and strategies for those both experiencing and witnessing online abuse. It was written with help from people who have been seriously affected by online harassment, including women, people of color, and members of the LGBTQ+ community.

StopBullying.gov
www.stopbullying.gov/
This official website of the U.S. government offers resources to help prevent all types of bullying, including cyberbullying.

Organizations

Crash Override
www.crashoverridenetwork.com
crashoverridenetwork.tumblr.com
twitter.com/CrashOverrideNW
Co-founded by Zoë Quinn, who was targeted during #GamerGate, Crash Override works with individuals affected by online harassment. The organization is an advocacy group and resource center for victims of online abuse. It works with companies, governments, and other professionals to stop cyber mobs. Crash Override provides resources for individuals, written guides, and referrals to other organizations that can provide victims with further aid.

Cyber Civil Rights Initiative (CCRI)
www.cybercivilrights.org
twitter.com/CCRInitiative
Created by a former victim of online harassment, the CCRI provides support for victims of cyber abuse. One of its goals is to raise public awareness and understanding about nonconsensual pornography. According to its website, the CCRI supports the development of better laws to protect against NCP while also supporting and respecting everyone's freedom of speech.

The Tyler Clementi Foundation
PO Box 345
Harrison, NJ 07029
twitter.com/TylerClementi
tylerclementi.org
The Tyler Clementi Foundation works toward ending harassment, bullying, and humiliation, both online and offline. It offers several programs and encourages individuals to use the internet in a positive way. The foundation's website offers many resources, including bullying statistics and a cybersafety guide.

Kate Mikoley is a writer and editor living in Sloan, New York. Prior to her start in children's publishing, she worked as a journalist in Upstate New York, reporting on community events and politics. In her spare time, she enjoys hiking, jogging, knitting, and attempting (sometimes successfully) to restore old furniture.